HOW CAN I HELP

ROXY
the
BUTTERFLY?

Frances Rodgers & Ben Grisdale

Editing, design and typesetting by UK Book Publishing

www.ukbookpublishing.com

ISBN: 978-1-8380019-3-3

HOW CAN I HELP

ROXY
the
BUTTERFLY?

Hello, my name is Roxy,
I am a butterfly and I
need your help.

I start my life as a caterpillar.

I go to sleep in my sleeping
bag in a dark place.

Then I begin to change.

ABRACADABRA

When I wake up, I have turned into a butterfly.

I like to feed on nectar from the flowers in your garden.

Please plant flowers for me. My favourite plant is called Buddleia, sounds like Bud-Lee-Ah.

I can taste through my feet.

When I am thirsty I like to drink juice from fruit.

Please put some old fruit out for me in your garden. I like bananas, oranges and apples.

My tongue is like a straw.

I get tired and need
somewhere to rest.

Please build me a bug hotel
out of sticks and wood.

Thank you for all your help.

Now that you know how to help *Roxy*, don't forget to help *Roly*, *Rory* and *Rosy* too!

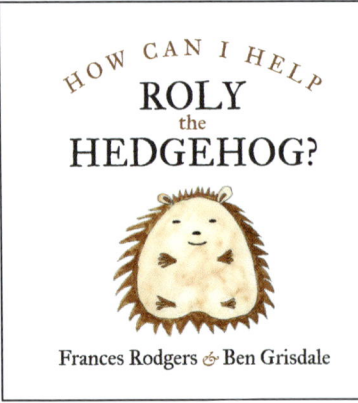

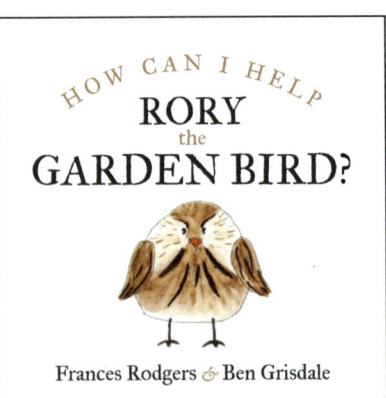

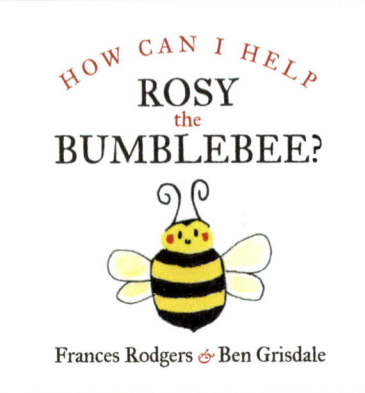

Available now on Amazon and other online retailers!

Printed in Poland
by Amazon Fulfillment
Poland Sp. z o.o., Wrocław